EVERYONE'S

Mandala

Coloring Book

Volume 2

By Monique Mandali

By the same author:
Everyone's Mandala Coloring Book (Volume 1)

First printing, August 1994
Second printing, May 1995
Third printing, September 1996

ISBN 1-56044-295-6

Printed in Mexico

Published by MANDALI PUBLISHING,
P.O. Box 21852, Billings, Montana 59104
(1-800-347-1223), in cooperation with SkyHouse Publishers,
an imprint of Falcon Press Publishing Co., Inc., Helena, Montana.

Design, typesetting, and other prepress work by
SkyHouse Publishers.

Distributed by Falcon Press Publishing Co., Inc.,
P.O. Box 1718, Helena, Montana 59624,
or call 1-800-582-2665.
Also distributed by
Bookpeople, New Leaf, Moving Books,
Pacific Pipeline, and Ingram.

Preface

When I was twenty-two, I had a prophetic dream.

It was one of those very short and vivid dreams whose last scene conveyed a message I have never forgotten. I saw myself at the edge of a sandy peninsula surveying an infinite expanse of water and knew instinctively that the Pacific Ocean stretched out on my left, the Atlantic Ocean on my right. I realized that I stood at the very place where these two huge bodies of water peacefully and willingly merged. A group of joyful children of all ages, skin colors, and ethnic backgrounds surrounded me on this particular journey. As they quieted, I told them very calmly and succinctly: "This is where East and West meet."

In more ways than one, the two mandala coloring books I created are an expression of my dream. The Swiss psychoanalyst Carl G. Jung called mandalas *archetypes* or universal symbols because every culture in the world reflects them in some form or other. Jung has since been joined by many scholars who believe that mandalas (whose Sanskrit root means both *center* and *circle*) are imprinted in our individual psyches. They represent our desire for wholeness regardless of our cultural and religious backgrounds, whether we are six years old or ninety, or are from Kenya, Brazil, China, Sweden, Australia, or Nepal. In mandalas, East and West do indeed meet.

THE MAGIC OF COLORING MANDALAS

As you leaf through this book, notice how some designs invite you to color them first. Trust your instincts. Surround yourself with a vast array of magic markers, crayons, or pencils and let your intuition guide you in how to color the page. You may want to personalize the mandala by drawing your own symbols inside some of the spaces. When you feel done, distance yourself a little. Look at your creation, absorb it, let it speak to you. It may suddenly occur to you what this colorful drawing reminds you of. Perhaps it is a vague yet familiar sense of another place, time, or ritual; maybe it mirrors your sense of connectedness; perhaps it simply reflects your current feelings of well-being, calmness, harmony, confusion, sadness, or anger. If you were to give this mandala a title, what would it be?

FUN WAYS TO USE MANDALAS WITH CHILDREN AND ADULTS

As coloring mandalas seems to have a very quieting and relaxing effect on us, they are perfect to take along on trips. Kids delight in them while traveling long distances by car, bus, or airplane. When I used to lived with friends in the middle of nowhere in Montana and occasional rain would turn the country roads into impassable and very slippery gumbo mud, kids and adults alike would sit in the family room and color mandalas hour after hour. The house would be decorated with our finished designs for days afterwards.

A friend of mine came up with the wonderful idea to use the mandala coloring book in a way that allows her to connect emotionally with significant people in her life. Loaning her copy of the book, she asked friends and relatives to color their favorite mandala, write something meaningful on the page, and attach a personal photo. The final product looks like a colorful photo album rich with metaphorical messages and portraits from those she loves.

MANDALAS IN THE CLASSROOM

Children seem to have an innate sense for mandalas and love to color them.

A grade school teacher I know designates one wall in her classroom as "the mandala wall." She starts each school year by asking her students to color a mandala of their choice and invites them to do so for the rest of the year whenever they have free time. They may display their creations on the wall, keep them in their desk, or take them home. Some children color the same design over and over again; others prefer to try different ones. She finds that when her students get too energetic, giving them a mandala to color quiets them down. She has also observed how this activity has an amazing calming effect on most children labeled with Attention Deficit Disorder, especially when they also listen to soothing music.

Once children become acquainted with mandalas, they may be encouraged to draw their own. Small, individually created mandalas can be strung together on a Christmas tree or hung as a mobile. One teacher asked her students to collectively create a huge chalk mandala on the playground around a specific theme, a task which involved teamwork as well as fun creativity.

COLORING MANDALAS TO PROMOTE HEALTH AND HEALING

Recent medical research has shown that the body's immune system and innate healing ability are enhanced when we are relaxed. As coloring mandalas appears to trigger the body's relaxation response, the book is a perfect gift for anyone recovering from an accident, surgery, or illness. It is also appreciated by adults who know the benefits of stress reduction and pain management exercises such as yoga or guided imagery, walking, gardening, knitting, or assembling puzzles.

A twenty-four-year-old friend who has been chronically ill since the age of two and has experienced many hospital stays since childhood recently commented: "This mandala coloring book should be in every children's hospital room." Yes, and it also has a place in all health care facilities and medical waiting rooms.

A UNIQUE GIFT

Whether for yourself or someone you love, mandala coloring books provide a pleasurable activity for people of any age. I continue to be interested in your personal or professional experiences with them and invite you to send me stories and anecdotes. I love reading them.

Thanks, and enjoy!

Monique Mandali

Monique Mandali, M.A., is a wholistic psychotherapist in Billings, MT, and author of two popular mandala coloring books. She uses the designs in her own practice and offers workshops for teachers, health care professionals, counselors in treatment centers, and anyone else interested in knowing more about the many uses of mandalas. (1-800-347-1223)

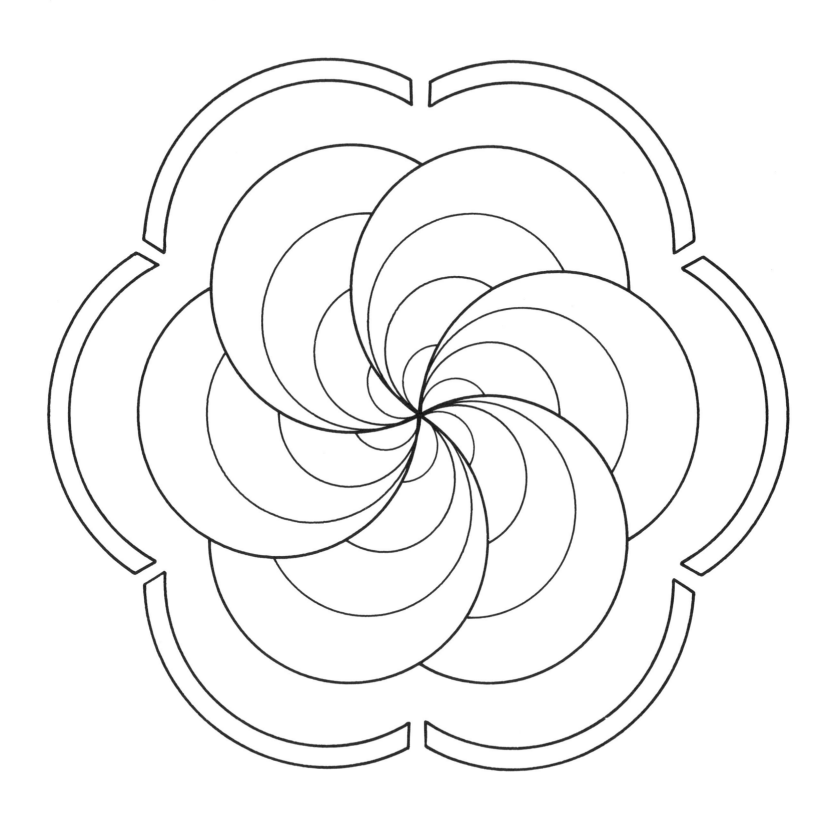